CHRISTIA

ERIC LIDDELL

Unit Study
Curriculum Guide

JANET & GEOFF BENGE

PUBLISHING
A Ministry Of Youth With A Mission
P.O. Box 55787, Seattle, WA 98155

YWAM Publishing is the publishing ministry of Youth With A Mission. Youth With A Mission (YWAM) is an international missionary organization of Christians from many denominations dedicated to presenting Jesus Christ to this generation. To this end, YWAM has focused its efforts in three main areas: 1) Training and equipping believers for their part in fulfilling the Great Commission (Matthew 28:19). 2) Personal evangelism. 3) Mercy ministry (medical and relief work).

For a free catalog of books and materials write or call:
YWAM Publishing
P.O. Box 55787, Seattle, WA 98155
(425) 771-1153 or (800) 922-2143
www.ywampublishing.com

Eric Liddell: A Unit Study Curriculum Guide
Copyright © 2001 by YWAM Publishing
Second printing 2001

Published by Youth With A Mission Publishing
P.O. Box 55787
Seattle, WA 98155

ISBN 1-57658-182-9

Verses marked KJV are taken from the King James Version of the Bible.

Verses marked NIV are taken from the Holy Bible, New International Version®, Copyright© 1973, 1978, 1984 by the International Bible Society. Used by permission of Zondervan Publishing House.

Printed in the United States of America.

Contents

Introduction...5

1. Key Bible Verses...8

2. Display Corner...11

3. Chapter Questions...13

4. Student Explorations...21

5. Community Links...27

6. Social Studies...32

7. Related Themes to Explore....................................40

8. Culminating Event..42

   Appendix A: Books and Resources.........................45

   Appendix B: Answers to Chapter Questions.............58

ERIC LIDDELL

1902–1945

Introduction

Eric Liddell:
A Unit Study Curriculum Guide

This unit study guide is designed to accompany the book *Eric Liddell: Something Greater Than Gold* from the Christian Heroes: Then & Now series by Janet and Geoff Benge. It provides the Christian school-teacher and homeschooling parent with ways to use the book as a vehicle for teaching or reinforcing various curriculum areas, including

- Creative writing.
- Drama.
- Movie critiquing.
- Reading comprehension.
- Essay writing.
- History and geography concepts.

As there are more ideas than could possibly be used in one unit, it is the parent/teacher's job to sift through the ideas and select those that best fit the needs of the students.

The activities recommended in this unit study guide are
- Reflective of a wide range of learning styles.
- Designed for both group and individual study.
- Suitable for a range of grade levels and abilities.

Learning Styles

Choose those activities that are best suited to your student or students. For example, when studying the physical features of a country, a kinesthetic learner will learn best by producing a three-dimensional clay model representing the physical features of the country, whereas a visual learner will find it more meaningful to produce a poster map of the country for the classroom wall.

Group or Individual Study

While the activities contained in this unit study guide are designed to be carried out by a student working alone, instructions are also provided for adapting an activity to a group situation.

Grade Levels/Abilities

As you thumb through this unit study guide, you will note that grade levels are not assigned to particular activities, though some areas, essay topics for example, progress from the simple to the complex. This approach has been taken because students of varying grade levels can undertake most of the activities. For example, one of the activities suggests a student make up a list of questions he or she would like to ask Eric Liddell and then use a tape recorder or video camera to create a mock interview. A fourth grader doing this activity would tend to ask concrete questions, such as "What was the food like in the internment camp?" or "What did you all do when you got bored?" In contrast, a ninth grader undertaking the same assignment would be able to ask more abstract questions, such as "Did you ever regret staying behind in China when your family left?" or "Why did you work so hard to help the children in the internment camp?" Each student uses the same activity and instructions to create work appropriate to his or her age and cognitive ability.

In the center of this unit study guide you will find two foldout pages. These pages contain three maps and a fact sheet to be filled out by the student. The maps and fact sheet are designed to be photocopied onto individual pages so that each student can store them in his or her folder. They are for use with the social studies section of this unit study guide (chapter 6).

Before you begin teaching from this unit study guide, please read through each section. You may wish to highlight the activities that appeal to you or that you know your students would enjoy or be challenged by. Many teachers find it useful to plan the culminating event (see chapter 8) first and then select a range of learning activities that lend themselves to this event.

For the sake of brevity in the instructions that accompany each section, the word *teacher* includes the homeschooling parent, and the word *student* refers to a child either in a traditional classroom or in a home-school environment.

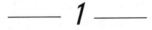

Key Bible Verses

The authors have selected four Bible verses that can be used alongside or as part of this unit study. For your convenience, these verses have been quoted in two versions: the King James Version and the New International Version. Of course, many other appropriate Bible verses can be added to the list if more are needed. The verses can be used in a number of ways. Four ideas for using them are listed below.

Memorization. The teacher can assign one or all of the verses to be memorized during the duration of the study. A chart could be made to track which students have completed memorizing which verses.

Meaning. The verses can be used to spark conversations on the spiritual aspects of Eric's life. This can then be translated into action by having students form groups and present one of the verses to the class in a creative manner. Students could make up a skit to illustrate the meaning of the verse or present a one-act play to show how the verse was relevant in the life of Eric Liddell.

Devotional. The teacher might also consider beginning a class or family devotional book. To do this, the teacher should familiarize the students with a variety of devotional writings and then ask them to write a devotion based upon their own understanding of one of the verses as it relates to the life of Eric Liddell. The pages could then be glued or copied into a blank book, illustrated, and signed. The various devotions could be read aloud at appropriate times, including during assemblies and family devotional times and at the culminating event.

Display. Students could also design a plaque, wall hanging, poster, or banner with one of the verses written on it. This could be hung in a prominent place while the unit study is being undertaken and used for decoration during the culminating event.

☙

❝A good name is rather to be chosen than great riches, and loving favour rather than silver and gold.**❞** (Proverbs 22:1 KJV)

❝A good name is more desirable than great riches; to be esteemed is better than silver or gold.**❞** (Proverbs 22:1 NIV)

☙

❝By this shall all men know that ye are my disciples, if ye have love one to another.**❞** (John 13:35 KJV)

❝By this all men will know that you are my disciples, if you love one another.**❞** (John 13:35 NIV)

❧

66Wherefore seeing we also are compassed about with so great a cloud of witnesses, let us lay aside every weight, and the sin which doth so easily beset us, and let us run with patience the race that is set before us, looking unto Jesus the author and finisher of our faith.99 (Hebrews 12:1–2a KJV)

66Therefore, since we are surrounded by such a great cloud of witnesses, let us throw off everything that hinders and the sin that so easily entangles, and let us run with perseverance the race marked out for us. Let us fix our eyes on Jesus, the author and perfecter of our faith.99 (Hebrews 12:1–2a NIV)

❧

66For bodily exercise profiteth little: but godliness is profitable unto all things, having promise of the life that now is, and of that which is to come.99 (1 Timothy 4:8 KJV)

66For physical training is of some value, but godliness has value for all things, holding promise for both the present life and the life to come.99 (1 Timothy 4:8 NIV)

— 2 —

Display Corner

Many students will enjoy collecting and displaying objects from the country or culture they are studying. It is motivational to designate a corner of the room, including a table or desk and wall space, that can be used for this purpose. Keep some index cards on the table and encourage students to label their contributions, including as much information as possible about where each object came from, what it is used for, and who would use it.

Encourage students to ask their parents and friends if they have anything interesting (but not valuable) from China that they could bring to class. A visit to a Chinese grocery could also yield some very interesting display items, as would a trip to the local library to find books on China and famous Chinese people and inventions. Following is a list of things students (or you) might like to display. Of course, there are many more options.

- A large map of China.
- Items of Chinese clothing (slippers, umbrellas, hats).
- Objects invented or discovered by the Chinese, such as an abacus, a magnet, fireworks (empty only), and noodles.
- Chinese food and food-related items, such as rice, millet, dried fish, noodles, pickled eggs, bowls, and chopsticks.
- Examples of Chinese writing, including Bibles and tracts. These are available through Chinese churches or by contacting the American Bible Society at (800) 32-BIBLE or online at www .americanbible.org.
- Photographs and articles about China, both in the past and in the present. (Use current events magazines and newspapers here.)
- Chinese coins.
- Chinese stamps.
- Chinese dolls in national dress.

3

Chapter Questions

There are four questions related to each chapter of *Eric Liddell: Something Greater Than Gold:*

1. A vocabulary question drawn from the text and referenced to a page in the book.
2. A factual question arising from the text.
3. A question to gauge the level of a student's comprehension.
4. An open-ended question seeking an opinion or interpretation.

These questions are designed for students to complete on their own. They are best answered as a student finishes reading each chapter in the book. Answers to the first three questions for each chapter are given in Appendix B. The answer to the fourth question is open-ended and needs to be evaluated separately. Since question four deals with a student's interpretation or opinions, it is a good question on which to base a group discussion. Keep in mind that there is no right or wrong answer to question four, just positions a student needs to justify.

To gain maximum benefit from the questions, the students should write full-sentence answers and not just one or two words. For example, in response to "Who started the Eric Liddell Fan Club?" they should write, "The fan club was started by Elsa McKechnie" rather than just "Elsa McKechnie."

Each vocabulary question asks the students to use the new word in a sentence. You have the option of having the students write a sentence using the new word. If you ask them to do this, make sure they write sentences that clearly demonstrate the meaning of the vocabulary word.

As a supplement to answering the questions, you may ask the students to write a short summary of each chapter or write a response to the chapter in their journal. This could involve the students writing about how they relate to Eric's actions, noting how they think they would react in a similar situation, and speculating as to what they think might happen next in the story.

Chapter One

1. What does mustered mean (page 13)? Use the word in a sentence.
2. By how much did Eric Liddell better the 400-meter record?
3. Why were Fitch and Imbach favorites to win the race?
4. What do you think thrilled the crowd more, the fact that Eric Liddell won the race or that he broke the world record? Why?

Chapter Two

1. What does tortuous mean (page 18)? Use the word in a sentence.
2. When was Eric Liddell born?
3. How did Eric earn the nickname "The Mouse"?
4. What effect do you think watching so many "old boys" going off to fight in the war might have had on young Eric? Why?

Chapter Three

1. What does recede mean (page 35)? Use the word in a sentence.
2. What did the Welsh (Wales) team do when the Scottish team beat them at rugby in 1922?
3. Why did DP think Eric Liddell would be useful in one of the Christian campaigns?
4. What do you think were some of the things Eric was thinking about when DP asked him to consider going on an evangelistic campaign with him?

Chapter Four

1. What does originated mean (page 49)? Use the word in a sentence.
2. When and where were the first modern Olympic Games held?
3. When Eric refused to run on Sunday, what steps did the British Olympic Committee take to change the situation?
4. Lord Cadogan told Eric that "to play the game is the only thing in life that matters" (page 51). If Eric had had the opportunity to respond to that statement, what do you think he might have said? Why?

Chapter Five

1. What does dubbed mean (page 56)? Use the word in a sentence.
2. How did the British masseur encourage Eric?
3. Why do most runners prefer to begin on the inside lane of the track and not the outside lane?
4. Do you agree with *The Bulletin* that Eric Liddell's win was a great achievement? Why or why not?

Chapter Six

1. What does donned mean (page 64)? Use the word in a sentence.
2. Where was Eric's final official race in the British Isles held?
3. What did Sir Alfred Ewing mean when he said, "Well, Mr. Liddell, you have shown that no one can pass you but the examiner"?
4. Why do you think Eric chose the quote, "In the dust of defeat as well as the laurels of victory there is glory to be found if one has done his best"?

Chapter Seven

1. What does dynasty mean (page 75)? Use the word in a sentence.
2. Name the three groups who were competing for power in China in 1925.
3. Why did the students at the Anglo-Chinese college go on strike?
4. How do you think the Chinese people might have viewed the foreign concessions in Tientsin?

Chapter Eight

1. What is a tripod (page 96)? Use the word in a sentence.
2. What made the annual International Athletic Games so special to Eric?
3. How did Eric earn the nickname "The Flying Scotsman"?
4. Why do you think Eric was able to forgive the photographer who cost him the race at the new stadium?

Chapter Nine

1. What does ordination mean (page 112)? Use the word in a sentence.
2. What surprised Eric when he returned to Edinburgh?
3. How did Eric cheer up the depressed man who sat next to him on the train?
4. Eric had said he would not run while he was in Scotland on furlough. Why do you think he made an exception for the students at Eltham College?

Chapter Ten

1. What does dejected mean (page 116)? Use the word in a sentence.
2. What was one good outcome of the military training the boys at the school had to have?
3. How did Eric know what the conditions were like in Siao Chang?
4. Do you think Eric should have gone to Siao Chang? Why or why not?

Chapter Eleven

1. What does torrential mean (page 125)? Use the word in a sentence.
2. What three armies attacked the villages in the area?
3. What were two ways Eric was able to help the hospital doctors?
4. What do you think would be the worst part about living around Siao Chang during this period?

Chapter Twelve

1. What does sabotaged mean (page 143)? Use the word in a sentence.
2. How did Eric hide the money for the coal?
3. What made him decide to take money instead of the coal back to Siao Chang?
4. What character traits would you say Eric showed in his efforts to bring coal to Siao Chang? Why?

Chapter Thirteen

1. What does ravages mean (page 149)? Use the word in a sentence.
2. Why did the Liddell family have to stay in the Red Cross center when they arrived in Nova Scotia?
3. What maneuver did the ships perform when they were being attacked by the U-boats? Why?
4. Up until he returned to China, what do you think was the most dangerous period in Eric's life? Explain why you think that.

Chapter Fourteen

1. What does hostility mean (page 165)? Use the word in a sentence.

2. What happened on December 7, 1941, that changed the United States' role in the war?
3. What problem did Eric's "Afternoon-Tea Church" solve?
4. What do you think Eric would have dreaded most about going to Weihsien Internment Camp? Why?

Chapter Fifteen

1. What does acquired mean (page 179)? Use the word in a sentence.
2. What were some of the countries that were represented in the internment camp?
3. What were some of the problems that Eric realized would have to be overcome to make the camp work?
4. Imagine you had spent your first day at Weihsien Internment Camp. What do you think would be the most difficult thing to adjust to?

Chapter Sixteen

1. What does monotony mean (page 186)? Use the word in a sentence.
2. How many words long were Eric's letters allowed to be?
3. Why did everyone laugh at Father Scanlan's punishment for smuggling?
4. What do you think were some of the things the children of Weihsien remembered most about Eric Liddell?

Chapter Seventeen

1. What does esteem mean (page 196)? Use the word in a sentence.

2. How long after Eric died did the United States Air Force arrive at Weihsien?

3. Why was Flo comforted when she learned how Eric had died?

4. Why do you think the Japanese guards let the internees surge through the gates? How else could they have reacted?

— 4 —

Student Explorations

Student explorations are a variety of activities that are appropriate to a wide range of learning styles. These activities consist of the following:

Essay Questions. These are questions that can be used as essay writing ideas. Students can either be assigned a topic or choose their own from the list. The simplest essay topics appear first, followed in order by those that are more complex.

Creative Writing. This includes writing such things as newspaper articles, poems, letters, resumés, songs, and journals.

Hands-On Projects. These are various kinds of projects, such as charts and graphs, models, comic strips, family crests, mottoes, dioramas, book covers, and mobiles.

Audio/Visual Projects. These involve such things as using a tape recorder to conduct a mock interview or to produce a radio play or commercial, or using still and video cameras to create dramatic presentations.

Arts and Crafts. These include art forms and crafts used in China.

Language Examples. Some examples of words written in Mandarin are given. Students can use these to make banners or placemats for the culminating event or in their hands-on projects. For example, they could use them around the edge of Eric Liddell's family crest.

[Note on group projects: All the suggestions described below are individual learning activities. However, some of the activities have bracketed paragraphs like this one after them that offer suggestions on how the activity can be adapted for class or group use.]

Essay Questions

1. Watch the movie *Chariots of Fire.* Write an essay highlighting the similarities and differences in story line between the book and the movie. Discuss why the differences may have occurred. (For insight into the process of turning Liddell's story into a movie, see *The Flying Scotsman* by Sally Magnusson.)

2. Imagine you have one hour to pack your belongings before you are taken to an internment camp. You are allowed to take a few clothes and ten other items. Write about what you would take and why.

3. Why do you think Eric Liddell was able to turn his back on fame and become a missionary to China? Give examples to back up your opinions.

4. Explain the ways that various wars impacted Eric Liddell's life.

Creative Writing

1. Choose a key event in Eric Liddell's life and write a newspaper article about it. For example, you might

report on Eric's refusing to run on Sunday at the Olympic Games or his decision to become a missionary to China or the news of his death. Be sure to include a catchy headline.

[Allocate different events to various students or groups of students and put them into a single newspaper format covering Eric Liddell's life.]

2. Write a poem about Eric Liddell that could have been read at his funeral service. Be sure to include the character traits people admired in him. Give the poem an appropriate title.

3. Imagine you are a teenager who was released from Weihsien Internment Camp. Write a letter to Florence Liddell and Eric's children describing your memories of "Uncle Eric."

4. Write a resumé for Eric Liddell to send to the principal of the Anglo-Chinese college in Tientsin to apply for a teaching position there. Be sure to mention educational background, work experience, awards and honors, and volunteer experiences.

5. Imagine you are Eric Liddell. Create a five-by-five grid in which twenty-five words can be written. Write a series of five letters (twenty-five words each) that try to give a picture of Eric's life in Weihsien Internment Camp. See how much information you can include in each letter.

Hands-On Projects

1. Make a timeline of Eric Liddell's life. Under it, record events of the Sino-Japanese War and the Second World War.

[Make a large timeline and have students write in-depth entries along it.]

2. Select or make models of five objects that represent various times in Eric Liddell's life. Make a display explaining why you consider the objects to be significant. For example, you might make a replica of a gold medal or weave a laurel wreath to represent Eric's achievement at the Olympic Games or find an old, battered hockey stick that could represent Eric's time in Weihsien.

    [Coordinate the "artifacts" and present them in a display. Have students prepare an audio tour of the artifacts telling how they reflect various aspects of Eric Liddell's life.]

3. While Eric Liddell was alive, comic books were drawn showing the main events of his life. Using the book, identify seven or eight of these main events and make your own comic page. (Students may wish to compare theirs with an original comic strip reproduced in *The Flying Scotsman.*)

4. Make a papier-mâché relief model of China and make "flags" to mark the various places Eric lived and worked.

5. Design a family crest or flag for Eric Liddell's family. What colors and symbols have you chosen? What have you placed in the center? Why? Explain your choices.

6. Create a Missionary Hall of Fame. Gather all the facts you can about Eric Liddell's physical appearance. Using a large piece of newsprint, draw a life-size picture of Eric. Along one side, write five or six facts that summarize the main events of his life.

[This can be done as a group project, or various students can do different missionaries. Display the finished picture in a hallway or library under a banner reading, "Missionary Hall of Fame."]

Audio/Visual Projects

1. Using a tape recorder or video camera, make up a mock interview in which you pretend to be Eric Liddell. Write a series of questions you think would be interesting to listeners and have someone read them to you. Answer them as you think Eric Liddell might have.

2. Create a version of *This Is Your Life* for Eric Liddell. Choose key people who would have known him and set up a studio where "Eric" can meet them again. Videotape your production.

Arts and Crafts

1. The Chinese were the first to invent paper. They used fibers from rags, tree bark, and plants and grasses such as hemp, bamboo, jute, and straw. Today there are many ways to make paper in the classroom or at home. Check your local library or bookstore for books that provide basic instructions on how to make paper.

2. The word *calligraphy* comes from the Greek words *kallos* and *graphos,* meaning "beautiful" and "writing." In China, calligraphy is a traditional art form as respected as painting or poetry writing. Calligraphy is traditionally done with a brush and ink on paper or silk. Check your local library or bookstore for books on the history and technique of

calligraphy. Practice writing the Mandarin words and phrases below.

Language Examples

Below are Chinese words and phrases written in Mandarin.

Always keep smiling.

China

missionary

You can also see examples of Chinese writing online at numerous websites. To find current sites, search using the key words "Chinese calligraphy."

── 5 ──

Community Links

Many communities have a rich supply of people and places to which students can be exposed to help them learn about and appreciate other cultures. It is well worth the effort to find out what your community has to offer with regard to the unit you are studying. For example, you might live near the site of an Olympic training facility or a Chinese church.

While it would be wonderful if you could take a field trip to visit some of these people and places, if you can't, it is often possible to have visitors come to the classroom. Whether you decide to take a field trip or invite a guest to your classroom, such activities need to be flanked by sound educational choices. Otherwise, much of the educational value of the event will not be realized. The following three steps will help students derive the greatest educational value from a field trip or classroom visit.

Step One: Preparation.

Students should always research the topic before they begin a classroom interview or field trip. In doing so they will be ready to ask intelligent questions based upon a sound knowledge of their topic. For example, if you are going to a Chinese church, the students should already know some of the history of the persecution of Christians in China. That way they can ask specific and interesting questions, such as "Do you have any contact with Christians in China today?" and "How is your church run in comparison to churches inside China?"

As the teacher, you need to give the students a clear idea as to why they are going on the field trip and what they are expected to produce with their findings. For example, you might say to them, "We are going to a Chinese church to hear the pastor tell us about the service and how the church is run. When we get back, we will split into groups, and you will be expected to produce a Venn diagram comparing and contrasting the Chinese church with a Western style church you are familiar with."

Students should be encouraged to compile lists of questions they want answers to, based upon what they have already learned. They should carry a clipboard with them to write down answers, draw sketches, and note observations. (For less motivated students, a simple worksheet of activities to be completed on the field trip itself can be a good idea.) Such activities reinforce the idea that the field trip is a serious educational event and that the student is there to gather information, not just to be a sightseer.

Step Two: The Event

During the field trip or classroom visit, make sure that the students remain on task. Insist that they be respectful of property and other people at all times. Make sure that you have a spokesperson designated to thank whomever you talk to as well as the parents who help with the event.

Step Three: Processing and Reflection

Students should be given time to process the information they have gathered from their field trip or classroom visit and reflect on it, both individually and as a class. This can take many forms, including making flow charts or diagrams of what they learned, editing interviews for articles or audiovisual presentations, writing reports, and making booklets. Something as simple as a class book called *Did You Know?,* in which each student writes down one fact he or she learned from the field trip, can serve as an effective reflection tool.

Suggested Community Links

Chinese Church. Locate a Chinese church in your area. Call the pastor and ask permission to take your class for a visit. (Attending a Sunday service would be ideal here if you could arrange it with the students' families.) Be sure to check to see whether the church has a dress code or any special customs the students (and you) should be aware of. If attending a Sunday service is not possible, ask if you can visit the pastor at church or if the pastor can come to school to speak to your class.

Chinatown. Perhaps you have a Chinatown in your area to visit. Here your students can get an idea of what living in China may be like. Have them listen carefully for people speaking to each other in Chinese and watch for Chinese customs that have been brought to America. If you do not have a Chinatown nearby, look for a general merchandise store or a Chinese grocery. (Be sure to have specific learning expectations in place before you go, or the field trip will become chaotic.)

Chinese People. People are some of the best resources of all. Are there any Chinese families in your neighborhood? Invite a member of the family to class and have the students learn about the family history from the person. How long has the family been in the United States? What happened to the family during World War II? What part of China is the family originally from? Has the person ever been back to China? Does he or she want to go back?

People Who Have Visited China. An increasing number of people have visited China. You may even be able to locate someone who has been on a mission trip or someone who has been a long-term missionary to Taiwan. If you find someone who fits either category, invite him or her to show slides or photos and other memorabilia from the trip.

Sports Facilities. Eric Liddell was an Olympic gold medalist. You probably won't have anyone as famous in your community, but you may have some very competitive runners or other athletes. Take a field trip to a local stadium or sports training center and ask an athlete how he or she trains for big events. (This will have to be arranged beforehand, of course.) What equipment does the athlete use? What is the current U.S. or world record in his or her event? What does the person wear to compete? How would he or she go about qualifying to compete in the Olympic Games in his or her sport? (In keeping with step one, your students should be able to answer these questions with regard to Eric Liddell, which can lead to some interesting comparisons.)

6

Social Studies

The social studies section is divided into five categories, each with suggestions on how to use the material given. The categories are briefly described below.

Places. This section covers significant places related to the story and named in the text of the book *Eric Liddell: Something Greater Than Gold.*

Journeys. This category covers journeys undertaken by Eric Liddell and his family as mentioned in the book.

Terms/Vocabulary. This section gives ideas for studying some of the terms used in the book.

Geographical Characteristics. This section contains suggestions for mapping some of the physical characteristics of China.

Conceptual Questions. This section provides the teacher with conceptual social studies questions related to the book.

Places

These places are categorized by country, with the page number where they are first referred to in the book given in parentheses. Students can undertake a range of activities with these place names. They can

- Locate and mark the places on the relevant country map. (Maps for this purpose are located in the foldout map section in the center of this guide.) Students may need to consult several maps (including historical maps) to find the locations of some of the lesser-known places mentioned.
- Note other points, such as their absolute location (latitude and longitude), and then observe how this location compares to other locations mentioned in the book. For example, calculate which location is closer to the equator or the North Pole.
- Calculate the relative locations of various places mentioned in the book. For example, how far is it from London to Tientsin or from Siao Chang to Weihsien?
- Construct a key to show population density in China.
- Explore how some of the place names have changed since the time of the story and give reasons for such changes.
- Pinpoint the places on a large wall map in the classroom. Students can then use index cards to write explanations as to why the various places are mentioned in the story. Each card could be pinned to the wall with a length of yarn connecting it to the appropriate place on the map.

Places in the United Kingdom

London (20)   Glasgow (36)
Dryman (20)   Armadale (36)
Loch Lomond (20)   Rutherglen (42)
Edinburgh (26)   Stoke-on-Trent (44)
Ben Nevis (28)   Liverpool (151)
Cardiff (34)

Places in China

Siao Chang (15)   Pei-tia-ho (79)
Shanghai (17)   Tehchow (142)
Peking (17)   Weihsien (167)
Tientsin (18)

Other locations

Paris, France (13)   Toronto, Canada (104)
The Hague, Holland (78)

Journeys

Using the following journeys, students can
- Map the journeys on the relevant map.
- Where possible, add details to the map from the
  story, such as how long each leg of the journey
  took, when Eric and his family started and finished their journeys, and the kinds of transpor-
  tation they used along the way.
- Compare the journeys Eric and his family took
  to taking the same journeys today. Students
  could research how they might reach those des-
  tinations today, how long it would take to get
  there, and how much it would cost.

Eric's journey

Eric visited or traveled through the following places on his journey overland from London, England, via Siberia, to Tientsin, China. (Students may need to look up the Trans-Siberian Railroad in an encyclopedia for help in plotting the exact route of this journey):

London, England (78)   Siberia (78)
The Hague, Holland (78)   Pei-tia-ho, China (79)
Russia (78)   Tientsin, China (81)
Ural Mountains (78)

The Liddell family's journey

The Liddell family visited or traveled through the following places on their journey from Scotland, via Canada, to Tientsin, China:

Liverpool, England (151)   Pacific Coast of Canada (150)
Irish Sea (151)   Pacific Ocean (150)
Atlantic Ocean (150)   Yellow Sea (82)
Nova Scotia, Canada (150)   Tientsin, China (82)
Toronto, Canada (150)

Terms/Vocabulary

Following is a list of terms used in the book. The page number where the term is first used is given in parentheses. The list covers a range of terms from the simple to the advanced. Students can use this list to

- Define and memorize the terms. You may find it helpful to asterisk or highlight in some way those terms you think would be appropriate for your students. If they know the meaning of all but five of the terms, have them learn only those five. Conversely, if they are unfamiliar with most of the terms, choose a realistic number for each student to explore and learn.

- Produce an individual or class reference book of terms. Assign each student a set number of terms to write a definition for or draw a sketch of. From this research, a book of definitions can be made, with one page allotted for each definition. This book could be added to throughout the year. (Students may need a dictionary to help them here.)
- Play reinforcement games such as *Go Fish*. To do this, draw some of the sketched definitions from the list compiled in the point above onto index cards and have the students take turns pairing them with written definitions.

Terms/vocabulary

Union Jack (13)	gale-force winds (116)
coastal plain (14)	tide (116)
irrigate (16)	droughts (125)
peasants (17)	crop yields (125)
Anglo-Chinese (48)	occupy (125)
channel (48)	dialects (127)
Olympic flag (51)	pidgin English (139)
republic (75)	territory (140)
warlords (76)	merchant vessel (150)
import (77)	convoys (150)
treaty (77)	quarantine (155)
Sino-Japanese (77)	garrison town (157)
peninsula (77)	internment camps (161)
massacre (80)	black market (171)
docks (82)	community (175)
topsoil (93)	consul (186)
horizon (102)	malnourished (191)

Geographical Characteristics

Be aware that some maps of China use different names for physical features and locations. Have students use an atlas to locate the following and then mark them on the blank map of China from the foldout map section in the center of this book:

- China's three major rivers, their sources, and their courses: the Yangtze River, the Huang Ho or Yellow River, and the Si Kiang or West River.
- The four major regions: North, Central, South China, and the Western Lands, including Tibet and the great desert basin.
- China's major mountain ranges: the Himalayas, the Pamirs, and the Tien Shan. Label the highest mountain in each range, giving its height.
- The following important cities: Sian, Lanchow, Beijing (Peking), Canton, Shanghai, Chungking, Nanking, Tientsin, Dairen, and Wuhan. Note the population of each city.
- The location of the Gobi Desert.
- The latitude and longitude lines that bisect China.
- The seas and oceans that border China: East China Sea, Yellow Sea, South China Sea, and the Pacific Ocean.
- The fourteen countries that share borders with China.
- The Great Wall of China.

Conceptual Questions

The following questions are ordered from the simple to the complex. You could ask the students to use these questions to

- Write one or more paragraphs to answer each question.
- Present an oral report to the class on one of the questions.
- Discuss the answers to a question or questions in a group context.

Questions to ponder

1. Locate and name two countries that are larger than China, two countries that are about the same size, and two countries that are a lot smaller.
2. How large is China compared to the United States? How does the population of China compare to the population of the United States?
3. Study China's largest cities. What natural feature or features are most of them located near? Why do you think this is?
4. Approximately one-fifth of the world's population lives in China. Using a map of the world, estimate how much of the world's land mass is in China. Is it more or less than one-fifth? What does this say about how densely populated China is?
5. Fourteen countries share borders with China. Using encyclopedias, newspapers, or other community resources, try to work out which of these countries have "friendly relations" with China and which do not.
6. Study a historical map of China and compare the names on it to the names on a modern map. See if you can discover why so many names have changed. What are other reasons why rivers and cities change their names? Research your own location. Did the

streets, stadiums, suburbs, towns, or rivers once have different names than they do today? Why did they change? (You may find older members of your community helpful here.)

7. Locate Taiwan. Research the problems that exist between Taiwan and mainland China and how they began.

Related Themes to Explore

Any unit study has natural links to many other topics that can also be explored. While it is impossible to pursue all such links in this context, the spoke diagram on the next page shows some related topics that students might find interesting to study alongside Eric Liddell.

There are two ways you might like to integrate some of these links into your classroom. Some teachers and parents have the flexibility to be able to choose the topics their students study and even to alter their selections partway through the year. If you are able to do this, use the theme wheel to help identify other topics you might like to follow up this unit with. For example, after studying Eric Liddell, your class could be interested in the history of the Olympic Games or the Sino-Japanese War.

Other teachers and parents are locked in to a less flexible curriculum. If this is your situation, you may still have the ability to change the order in which various topics are taught. Look through the topics listed to see whether any coincide with topics you have already scheduled for later in the year. Consider the possibility of scheduling the teaching of these topics closer to this unit so that cross-curriculum learning can take place.

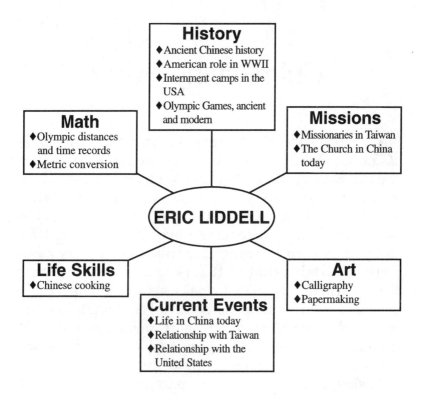

--- *8* ---

Culminating Event

As adults, we like to have a reason to learn some-thing. We learn a new computer program so that we can balance our checking account, a song so that we can sing it at a wedding, or the rudiments of another language so that we are able to find our way around in a foreign country. Students have the same need for purpose in their learning. It is valid but not very moti-vational to tell a student that he or she needs to gather and learn information to pass a test or move up a grade. It is much more motivational for a student when he or she has some other, more meaningful goal in mind. This goal can be a specific forum through which each student can express his or her newly acquired knowledge. We believe that part of the role of the teacher is to provide such a forum, which we call the culminating event.

As the name implies, the culminating event marks the end of the unit study and gives a sense of closure to the topic. It also serves to put what students have learned into a larger context that can then be shared with others.

The culminating event can be as simple as inviting the class next door (or the homeschooled children down the street) to come and hear poems and stories and view the written work that students have completed. Conversely, it could be as involved as hosting a parent/ neighborhood dinner featuring Chinese food, songs, games, plays, and presentations on the life and achievements of Eric Liddell and the places where he served.

No matter how simple or elaborate the culminating event is, make sure you have the broad outline of it in mind before planning the other activities for your unit study, as the two are integrally linked.

Idea Sparks

Food. Prepare and serve regional food. Fruits and vegetables grown and eaten in the Shantung and Hopei regions include pears, peaches, apples, grapes, melons, peanuts, leeks, and onions. Meats eaten in the region include roast chicken, roast pork, prawns, and freshwater crab. Steamed bread and millet are more commonly served than rice.

A typical celebration meal from this region might include steamed bread; steamed vegetables, including leeks, onions, and garlic; and boiled, roasted, or barbecued chicken or pork. The meat, which is cut into chunks, would be accompanied by bowls of dipping sauces. Some common sauces are chili-soy sauce, garlic-vinegar mix, Haisen sauce, plum sauce, and sweetened soy jam.

Provide chopsticks and Chinese tea served in bowls and eat off a low table or the floor.

Music. Play traditional Chinese music in the background to set the mood. (Many libraries stock ethnic music selections.) Students may also enjoy listening to the British National Anthem, "God Save the King/Queen."

Oral Presentations. Present poems, essays, reports, speeches, reviews, and devotions that students have written during the course of the unit study.

Display. Display other work, including artwork, map work, models, newspapers, and video interviews.

Clothing. Younger students might enjoy dressing up in Chinese outfits for this event.

Cultural Activities. Play traditional Chinese children's games.

Appendix A

Books and Resources

This appendix is divided into six sections: (1) other biographies of Eric Liddell, (2) related books, (3) related documentary and movies, (4) other books in the Christian Heroes: Then & Now series set in China, (5) related articles from *National Geographic,* and (6) Internet site.

Some of the books listed here are more difficult to get copies of than others. If they are not available at your local Christian bookstore, many of the titles can be located in secondhand bookstores (try using the Internet to locate them). Most of the titles are also available through the national interlibrary loan service.

Other Biographies of Eric Liddell

All the biographies listed on the bibliography page of *Eric Liddell: Something Greater Than Gold,* as well as others that may be of interest, are listed here. Each listing has basic information on how to locate the book, including its ISBN number. The approximate age level

of the intended reader is also given, along with the
number of pages in each book and some comments to
help you decide whether you might want to include
this book in your unit study. All of the books about Eric
Liddell are written at a higher reading level than the
books in the Christian Heroes: Then & Now series and
would be interesting for a teacher to read for his or her
own information and as background for the unit. Keep
in mind that children learn best by example, so consider choosing one good adult biography to read and
enrich your own understanding of the topic.

TITLE: *Scotland's Greatest Athlete:*
              The Eric Liddell Story
Author: D. P. Thomson
Publisher: The Research Unit, Crieff, Perthshire, 1970
ISBN: N/A
Age Level: Adult, 240 pages

Synopsis: This biography of Eric Liddell is written by the
man who encouraged him to speak publicly at his first
Christian meeting. It covers many details of Eric's life,
including details on his running accomplishments. It also
deals extensively with the various ways Eric Liddell's life
was honored and remembered after his death.

Comments: This book jumps around in time a little and
would not be interesting read-aloud material for a student.
However, if someone is interested in the records Eric broke
and the progression of his athletic career, they are all cov-
ered thoroughly in the book.

TITLE: *Complete Surrender*
Author: Julian Wilson
Publisher: Monarch, 1996

ISBN: 1854243489
Age Level: Adult, 150 pages

Synopsis: This is a mature biography of Eric Liddell. It tells the story of both his spiritual and athletic development.

Comments: The book has twenty-two photos showing Eric Liddell at different times in his life. This would be a good choice for a teacher to read for his or her own interest.

TITLE: *Eric Liddell* (Men of Faith Series)
Author: Catherine Swift
Publisher: Bethany House, 1990
ISBN: 1556611501
Age Level: Adult (easy reading), 176 pages

Synopsis: This is another thorough biography of Eric Liddell. The story is well told, with an emphasis on the social and political climate of China before and during Eric's lifetime. It spends longer on Eric's early life, and one final chapter takes the reader from Siao Chang through to his death.

Comments: This would be a great book for a teacher to read alongside the students. It is well written and detailed, except for Eric's time in the Weihsien Internment Camp, which is very sketchy.

TITLE: *The Flying Scotsman*
Author: Sally Magnusson
Publisher: Quartet Books, 1982
ISBN: 0704333791
Age Level: Adult, 192 pages

Synopsis: This biography has a first and a last chapter about why the movie *Chariots of Fire* was made. It makes references to the movie throughout the book. Especially interesting are the places where the author points out the differences between the true story and the movie and relates the reasons these changes were made. The book includes extensive writing about Weihsien Camp and Eric Liddell's role in it, as well as many quotes from other internees about him. It also gives a lot of information about his funeral services.

Comments: Contains fourteen photographs, including a reproduction of a comic strip that was made about Eric. This is an interesting book for an adult or older student to read, particularly if you intend for the class to watch *Chariots of Fire*. It might be very informative to read portions of the book aloud about why producer David Puttnam chose to make the movie and Ian Charleson's reactions to playing the role of Eric (see Related Documentary and Movies).

Related Books

This section contains a list of other books that complement the topics in this unit study. This includes books about other people's experiences in Japanese internment camps. Again, ISBN number, age level, and relevant comments are included for each book listed.

Of course, there are many other books that relate in some way to this unit study. You may want to record inside the back cover of this guide the titles of other books you find particularly helpful.

TITLE: *Courtyard of the Happy Way*
Author: Norman Cliff
Publisher: Arthur James Ltd., 1977
ISBN: 0853051917

Age Level: This book is appropriate in content and reading level for the same readership as *Eric Liddell: Something Greater Than Gold.*

Synopsis: Norman Cliff was born in China in 1925. He was the son of third-generation missionaries to China. (His great-grandmother's brother was Hudson Taylor.) *Courtyard of the Happy Way* begins with a description of life at the famous China Inland Mission boarding school in Chefoo. Cliff was an eighteen-year-old just finishing high school when the Japanese relocated the Chefoo school students to Weihsien. He spent two years there before finally being released.

Comments: This very readable book gives a wonderful window into life during the Sino-Japanese War through the eyes of a child. Enough detail is given to make it interesting, and it makes several references to Eric Liddell.

TITLE:	*A Boy's War*
Author:	David Michell
Publisher:	Overseas Missionary Fellowship Press, 1994
ISBN:	9971972719

Age Level: The material in this book is appropriate to an eight- to twelve-year-old level, but the reading level itself is twelve to fourteen years. It is well written and funny in places and would make a good book to read aloud to younger students, either in its entirety or portions of it. 176 pages.

Synopsis: David Michell was another missionary child who was a student at Chefoo. He was eleven when he was sent to Weihsien Camp. The book describes in detail his time in school and his time in Weihsien Camp. The last chapters record Michell's trip in 1985 with several other ex-internees back to the site of the camp.

Comments: This book has some good photographs of the camp and reproduces some interesting documents and correspondence relating to the story. It makes extensive references to Eric Liddell.

TITLE: *Shantung Compound: The Story of Men*
              and Women Under Pressure
Author: Langdon Brown Gilkey
Publisher: HarperCollins, 1991
ISBN: 0060631120

Age Level: Definitely adult in reading level and content. However, there are some very funny stories that students would enjoy having read to them. 242 pages.

Synopsis: Langdon Brown Gilkey was a young teacher in Tientsin when he was transferred to Weihsien. He kept a detailed diary, which he reconstructed to give a picture of the day-to-day life inside the compound. The book covers the two years of internment in great detail, including the liberation of the camp. Gilkey later went on to become a professor of theology at University of Chicago Divinity School.

Comments: This book describes adult concepts and situations. It gives a less-than-flattering view of many of the missionaries, but Gilkey is very positive in his memories of Eric Liddell (whom he calls Eric Ridley, as all names in the text have been changed to protect individuals).

TITLE: *We Signed Away Our Lives: How One Family*
              Gave Everything for the Gospel
Author: Kari Torjesen Malcolm
Publisher: InterVarsity Press, 1990
ISBN: 0830817182
Age Level: Adult (easy reading), 184 pages

Synopsis: Kari Torjesen Malcolm was born in 1925 to Nor-wegian parents who were working in China with China Inland Mission. The book tells the story of her family's life, beginning with her father's call to missionary work, and her family's eventual return to China. Kari Torjesen Malcolm and her brothers were interned in Weihsien soon after learning that their father had been killed in a Japanese bombing raid.

Comments: This book chronicles a family's faith and calling from one generation to the next. It is simply and powerfully written.

Related Documentary and Movies

Listed in this section are a documentary and movies that have been made about the life of Eric Liddell or issues that have some relationship to events in his life. The rating for each movie is included, but as with all unfamiliar material, it is prudent to preview them before showing them to the class.

Movies and documentaries are particularly useful in showing the visual details of another place and time period. As students watch, encourage them to study the clothing, weather, crops, terrain, and other geo-graphical factors shown in the movie or documentary.

TITLE: *China: A Century of Revolution (Part One)*
Director: Sue Williams
Type: Documentary
Length: 120 minutes
Year: 1989

Comments: This is an excellent documentary on China from 1911 to 1949. It uses a lot of original footage and interviews with survivors of that period. It gives a clear timeline of the events that affected Eric Liddell's life and led to the Communist takeover. You might want to show selections of this video, since it is so long, though it would hold the attention of the serious history student. It contains two graphic execution scenes, many dead bodies, and some partial nudity.

TITLE:	*Chariots of Fire*
Director:	Hugh Hudson
Type:	Movie, drama
Length:	123 minutes
Year:	1981
Rated:	PG

Comments: This Academy Award–winning movie is about Eric Liddell and his involvement in the 1924 Olympic Games.

TITLE:	*Empire of the Sun*
Director:	Steven Spielberg
Type:	Movie, drama
Length:	152 minutes
Year:	1987
Rated:	PG

Comments: This is the story of a young British boy, Jim Graham, who finds himself alone in a Japanese internment camp. While it is a realistic portrayal of life in an internment camp, you will want to preview it to see whether it is suitable for your students.

Other Christian Heroes: Then & Now Books Set in China

TITLE:	*Hudson Taylor: Deep in the Heart of China*
Authors:	Janet and Geoff Benge
Publisher:	YWAM Publishing, 1998

ISBN: 1576580164
Age Level: 10 years and up, 208 pages

Comments: Hudson Taylor (1832–1905) was one of the first missionaries to China. He persevered through personal tri-als, including the death of his first wife and three of his children. Eventually he founded the China Inland Mission.

TITLE: *Gladys Aylward: The Adventure of a Lifetime*
Authors: Janet and Geoff Benge
Publisher: YWAM Publishing, 1998
ISBN: 1576580199
Age Level: 10 years and up, 208 pages

Comments: Gladys Aylward (1902–1970) overcame a poor childhood and meager education to become the first for-eigner ever to be granted citizenship by the Chinese govern-ment. Her life is filled with almost unbelievable adventures, such as mediating between rioters in a Chinese prison, befriending and converting a high-ranking mandarin, and leading nearly one hundred children over rugged, enemy-filled mountains to safety during the Sino-Japanese War. Note: Gladys Aylward and Eric Liddell were born the same year, though Gladys Aylward served farther inland than Eric Liddell.

TITLE: *Jonathan Goforth: An Open Door in China*
Authors: Janet and Geoff Benge
Publisher: YWAM Publishing, 2000
ISBN: 1576581748
Age Level: 10 years and up, 208 pages

Comments: Jonathan Goforth (1859–1936) felt called to China after his conversion. He soon gained the reputation as China's greatest evangelist, addressing crowds of up to twenty-five thousand. Jonathan and his wife, Rosalind, equipped their home with "Western conveniences" and then opened it up for tours. More than one thousand people toured the house each day, and many stayed after the tour to hear Jonathan preach. Even after he became blind, Jonathan continued to travel and preach.

TITLE: *Lottie Moon: Giving Her All for China*
Authors: Janet and Geoff Benge
Publisher: YWAM Publishing, 2001
ISBN: 1576581888
Age Level: 10 years and up, 208 pages

Comments: Lottie Moon (1840–1912) was born into a wealthy and privileged family in pre–Civil War Virginia. She gained her master of arts degree, becoming the most educated woman in the South. Lottie left America in 1873 and spent the next thirty-nine years in China. On the two occasions she returned to the United States on furlough, Lottie Moon stirred the Southern Baptists to give so much money to foreign missions that after she died, a Christmas missionary offering was taken up in her name. This practice continues today.

Related National Geographic Articles

Many magazines contain articles related to this unit study. We have chosen to reference *National Geographic* because it can provide contemporaneous commentary on many events, since it dates back to the 1880s, and because it is widely available in libraries and schools throughout the country.

These articles and their accompanying photographs represent just some of those available that bear on aspects of Eric Liddell's life. They can be used in a variety of ways to support and reinforce this unit study. For example, you could have students analyze how accurate the author of the article "The Chinese Boxers" was in his predictions about China's political future (July 1900). After reading the article about foreigners and treaty ports in China, your students could draw a graph depicting the number and ratios of foreigners in China. Your students could also contrast the internment camp experience of the writer of the article "Today on the China Coast" (February 1945) with that of Eric Liddell.

Articles on China from 1900–1919

These articles were published around the time Eric Liddell was born in China.

TITLE: The Chinese Boxers
Issue Date: July 1900, pages 281–287

Description: An article about the rising Boxer movement from a Western viewpoint. It talks about why missionaries were killed.

TITLE: Foreigners and Foreign Firms in China
Issue Date: August 1900, page 330–332

Description: A breakdown of the numbers of each foreign population in the treaty ports.

TITLE: Curious and Characteristic Customs of China
Issue Date: September 1910, pages 791–806

Description: A very readable account of a reporter's impressions of Chinese life and customs.

TITLE: Shantung—China's Holy Land
Issue Date: September 1919, pages 231–252

Description: Lots of good photographs and text about life in Shantung Province.

Articles on China from 1932–1945

These articles were published around the time of Eric Liddell's return to China to work as a missionary.

TITLE: Raft Life on the Hwang Ho
Issue Date: June 1932, pages 743–752

Description: Gives some good insight into both the conditions and kinds of boats Eric Liddell would have encountered as he traveled through the region.

TITLE: Cosmopolitan Shanghai, Key Seaport of
             China
Issue Date: September 1932, pages 311–336

Description: An excellent look at the concept of concessions, along with photographs.

TITLE: Coastal Cities of China
Issue Date: November 1934, pages 601–643

Description: A wonderful introduction to the coastline of China, particularly with regard to foreign trade and traffic.

TITLE: 6,000 Miles Over the Roads of Free China
Issue Date: March 1944, pages 355–384

Description: A firsthand account of a journalist who spent five months in the interior of war-torn China, reporting on everything from orphans to politics.

TITLE: Today on the China Coast
Issue Date: February 1945, pages 217–238

Description: The author of this article talks about Pei-tia-ho and Tientsin as well as his time in a Japanese internment camp.

Article about the Olympic Games

TITLE: Let the Games Begin
Issue Date: July 1996, pages 42–69

Description: An interesting overview of the history of the ancient and modern Olympic Games.

Article about Scotland during the time of Eric Liddell

TITLE: Edinburgh, Athens of the North
Issue Date: August 1932, pages 219–246

Description: Stories about Edinburgh's long history. Includes photographs of people and places Eric Liddell would have been familiar with.

Internet Site

www.eric-liddell.org

This very informative website shows the work that is being done in Scotland today by the Eric Liddell Foundation. It also provides information about Eric's life. Of particular interest is a section titled "Recollections of Eric," in which ten people write about their memories of Eric Liddell. The biographical notes on Eric contain six photographs of him and his family.

Appendix B

Answers to Chapter Questions

Chapter One

1. Mustered means to have gathered up.
2. He bettered the 400-meter record by two-tenths of a second.
3. Fitch and Imbach were favorites because they had both broken the world record in the 400 meters.

Chapter Two

1. Tortuous means filled with twists and turns.
2. Eric was born on January 16, 1902.
3. He earned the nickname by playing the part of the mouse in the school play *Alice in Wonderland.*

Chapter Three

1. Recede means to move backward or away from.
2. The Welsh team honored Eric Liddell and Leslie Gracie by carrying them around the park after the game.

3. Eric was a well-known member of the Scottish rugby team, and DP thought he would appeal to hard-working men more than an ordinary student would.

Chapter Four

1. Originated means to have begun.
2. The first modern Olympic Games were held in 1896 in Athens.
3. The committee met with the Olympic organizers, but the organizers would not change Eric's running dates. Then the committee reassigned Eric to other racing distances.

Chapter Five

1. Dubbed means to have renamed something.
2. To encourage Eric, the masseur sent him a note at his hotel with a quote from the Bible on it.
3. Most runners prefer the inside lane because they can see where their opponents are and how fast they are running. Also, it is often easier to catch up to someone than stop a runner from overtaking you in this lane.

Chapter Six

1. Donned means to have put something on.
2. Eric's last official race in Britain was held in Hampden Park, Glasgow.
3. One sense of "pass" is to graduate someone from a program or exam. Another meaning is to move beyond someone. Ewing made a play on words to emphasize Eric's unbeatable presence on the track.

Chapter Seven

1. A dynasty is a series of rulers who all belong to the same family.
2. The three groups competing for power inside China in 1925 were the warlords, the Nationalists, and the Communists.
3. The students went on strike because during a demonstration, British forces in Shanghai had fired on Chinese students, killing one of the demonstrators. After the incident, students boycotted the Anglo-Chinese college in protest.

Chapter Eight

1. A tripod is a three-legged stand.
2. The games were so special to Eric because it was the first time his entire family had been there to watch him run.
3. He earned the nickname when he jumped onto a boat that was nearly fifteen feet out from the wharf. A reporter saw him and coined the name.

Chapter Nine

1. Ordination is a ceremony to officially recognize a pastor or priest.
2. Eric was surprised by the number of people who remembered him and wanted to hear or see him.
3. To cheer the man up, Eric gave him a letter written by Bella Montgomery.

Chapter Ten

1. Dejected means to be sad or depressed.

2. The boys began to think about their religious beliefs, and many of them joined Bible studies as a result.

3. Eric's brother, Robert, who worked at the hospital in Siao Chang, wrote to him about the conditions there.

Chapter Eleven

1. Torrential means coming down in a rushing stream of water.

2. The Japanese, Nationalist, and Communist armies attacked the villages.

3. Eric was able to help the doctors by telling them where the fighting was heavy and what type of injuries to expect and by bringing the wounded to the hospital.

Chapter Twelve

1. Sabotaged means to have secretly destroyed something belonging to the enemy to make it more difficult for them to carry out their plans.

2. Eric hid the money in a loaf of French bread.

3. When he tried to take the coal, it was stolen from him, but he thought he could hide the money and take it back.

Chapter Thirteen

1. Ravages means the damaging effects of something.

2. The family stayed in the Red Cross center because the girls were quarantined with measles.

3. The ships would zigzag to become harder targets for the U-boats to hit.

Chapter Fourteen

1. Hostility means showing extreme dislike for someone or something.
2. On December 7, 1941, the Japanese bombed Pearl Harbor, Hawaii, bringing the United States into the war.
3. Eric's "Afternoon-Tea Church" was formed to get around the rule that no more than ten foreigners were allowed to meet together in one place.

Chapter Fifteen

1. Acquired means to have obtained something.
2. At least fifteen countries were represented at the camp, including Italy, Belgium, Holland, India, Palestine, Russia, and Cuba as well as Great Britain and the United States.
3. Eric identified several problems: the many languages spoken in the camp, the number of people who were used to having servants, the broken condition of everything, and the number of school-age children with nothing to do.

Chapter Sixteen

1. Monotony means a boring and repetitive state.
2. The letters could be twenty-five words long.
3. Everyone laughed at Father Scanlan's punishment because he was a Trappist monk who was used to living in total silence.

Chapter Seventeen

1. Esteem means to value something or someone.
2. The camp was liberated six months after Eric died.

3. Flo was comforted because she knew that Eric did not die as a result of living in the camp or because he did not have adequate medical attention.